Paper Wings

The Collected Poetry of Betty Dobson

Second Edition

InkSpotter Publishing

Paper Wings

The Collected Poetry of Betty Dobson

PUBLISHED BY INKSPOTTER PUBLISHING
163 Main Avenue, Halifax, Nova Scotia, Canada B3M 1B3
http://inkspotter.com/

Copyright © 2006 Betty Dobson

All rights reserved. No part of this publication may be reproduced, stored in a retrieval system, or transmitted in any form or by any means electronic, mechanical, photocopying, recording or otherwise, without the prior written permission of the publisher.

Printed and bound in the United States of America by CreateSpace

---

Library and Archives Canada Cataloguing in Publication

Dobson, Betty, 1962-
  Paper wings : the collected poetry of Betty Dobson.

ISBN 978-0-9739896-1-8

  I. Title. II. Title: Collected poetry of Betty Dobson.

PS8607.O369P36 2006   C811'.6   C2006-905250-6

To Mum and Dad, who always told me
"You can't make a living at that"—
thanks for giving me a big enough
stubborn streak to try anyway

Contents

Acknowledgements iii
Introduction v

Paper Wings 1
Peep Hole 2
Stars Stutter 4
Faded Rose Tattoo 5
The Verge 6
The Passionate Mama's Boy 7
The Lilac Room 8
Gagetown Reflexes 9
Last Hunt Over Bras d'Or 10
Elvis Clones 11
Thin Wires 12
Closer Now 13
Baddeck 14
Supplication 15
The Night She Left 16
Wisdom Flowers 17
Dreamcatcher 18
Window on a Taos Day 19
Mist 20
The Last Time I Saw Lisa 21
Evening Sounds 22
Knowledge and Memory 23
Seaforth on the Atlantic 24
Scrape, Rattle, Bang 25
Grandfather Waltzes 26
Fallen Seasons 27
Unfinished Portrait 28
Magenta Skin 29
Light Bright on High 30
White Feathers 31
Surfer Joe 32
Listening Post 34

Restoration Piece 35
Monarch 36
Born in Black 37
For the Lost 38
No Sparks 39
Annie Laurie's Parting Gift 40
Fishing! 41
William Shakespeare, Astronaut 42
At the Outset 43

Acknowledgements

The greatest thanks go to my poetry teacher, Brian Bartlett, for helping me sift through some less-than-stellar early efforts to discover the true poetry waiting within.

The poems within this slim volume have all been published in one form or another. I thank everyone involved in the following publications for having faith enough in my writing to allow me into their worlds.

Journals (print and electronic):

52%
The Womyn's Centre, Carleton University

Amaze: The Cinquain Journal
http://www.amaze-cinquain.com/

Apollo's Lyre
http://apollos-lyre.com/

Book Lover's Haven
Chistell Publishing

Nova Scotia, Canada
http://www.novascotiacanada.info/

Outspoken Art/Arte Claro
http://outspokenart.withtheworks.net/

Sol Magazine
http://www.sol-magazine.org/

Anthologies:

The Binnacle Second Annual Ultra-Short Competition 2005
The Binnacle Third Annual Ultra-Short Competition 2006
The University of Maine at Machias

Body Language: A Head-to-Toe Anthology
Black Moss Press

Check the Rhyme: An Anthology of Female Poets & Emcees
Lit Noire Publishing

Epiphanies and Other Absurdities
The Writers' Association

Facing Faces 2001-04: Eres el amor de mi vida
Coalition of Artists United for Social Engagement

Passing
PoetWorks Press

Satire of the Inanities
The Writers' Association

Introduction

I've never been comfortable writing about myself, except maybe in the pages of my journal, so writing this introduction has been a somewhat daunting task.

Then I remind myself that the introduction is more about the book than about me. If you've picked up *Paper Wings*, you probably want to know about the poetry inside.

These poems were written during the past dozen or so years. Some came out of university poetry classes. Others grew from great and lesser loves. And a few spewed forth during downright wacky moments that might never come again...at least not in the same form.

While I've often hesitated to thrust my little darlings out into the big old world, each and every poem in this book has had at least some experience with public scrutiny. And I'm pretty sure each and every one has tasted its share of rejection. Perhaps some will again.

That, I leave to you to decide.

Paper Wings

I grew up with a love of words,
Reading all my mind could hold:
A traveler to far flung lands,
Soaring on paper wings.

Reading all my mind could hold,
I felt the words push out again,
Soaring on paper wings
Over worlds of my design.

I felt the words push out again,
Alive and ripe for sharing
Over worlds of my design,
Mapped without border lines.

Alive and ripe for sharing,
A traveler to far flung lands,
Mapped without border lines—
I grew up with a love of words.

Peep Hole

Thump
on the door. Just the
Sears Christmas Wish Book
or Canadian Tire?

For once, you respond—
relaxed
but city-conditioned
to venture

a peep.
As always, the hallway stretches away
farther than fact,
like a passenger-side mirror.

Bright yellow
hovers by the faded
silver gleam of an elevator door.
Quarter-turn clockwise

releases the catch. You
look out
long enough to see
empty floor and the

nearer, clearer
shoulder curve just past the
stairwell exit.
Another tenant on his way

out? Back in and click
and thoughts of dinner
and one more revision
while time still allows.

Turn back.
Whispered sense leads the eye
back to the peep hole.
Yellow jacket

already closer
than the unaided
eye would allow.
He winds his way,

reaching at your end for the waist-
level handle.
No warning rattle, just the
slow, silent

rise and fall
that matches your
breathing.
Or is that his?

Stars Stutter

the stars
stutter in code—
ancient plea or warning—
falling from heaven to earth on
blind eyes

Faded Rose Tattoo

she's like her faded rose tattoo
youth's sigil on her breast
paled from the centre
colour worn away
with the flesh
petals fallen
or plucked
in fits of love
<love me not>
her withered stem
bowed before time
and distended leaves
courted only by gravity
tempted by the blade
pruning and grafting
(winter's harbinger)
like wiring the bud
for two more days'
worth of show, illusion
cast in a rose-cut image

The Verge

tangy
scent of regret
drifts through open windows
autumn night on the verge of cold
farewell

The Passionate Mama's Boy

Come live with me, be my lover—
Take no notice of my mother.
Just give her time, she'll hold you dear;
Besides, she's hardly ever here.

Between her job and her "friends"
Her busy schedule never ends.
You can rearrange the pots and pans,
Clean the cupboards, recycle cans.

Cook whatever suits your palate;
Feed me steak, tofu, or carrot.
I promise you'll receive a treat
Of flowers, fun, or something sweet.

I have nothing, love, without you
Except my butane barbecue.
Bring your cat, your books, your broom;
We'll let you have your own bedroom.

On nights when I'm not working late—
As long as mother's on a date—
We'll find a sitter for the cat
And overturn the welcome mat.

Believe in me, my offer's true—
I've had three years to think this through.
Don't take too long, please, to decide;
I've got to run and catch my ride.

The Lilac Room

The Lilac Room lulls me with its
vibrancy. Clapping leaves and early
evening sun blend along the wall,
fluttering there like lambent heartbeats.
purple hearts cry out for new tortures.
shiftless, drifting clouds smother the
rhythm, like sailors turned away on
outbound ships. Hearts change again
and again this side of the horizon.

Gagetown Reflexes

The tiny flame flickers and fights to keep burning, but slowly
dies. A red ember remains on the wick, glowing, then goes out.
She has no fear of the night—her bunker of silence and peace.
The odd car whispers by as rain taps on the window, lonely, excluded.
Black softens to grays, shifting as if alive. She watches from bed,
rapt by the shapes that form and vanish with each breath she takes.

The old radiator breaks through the silence—a harsh rhythm.
Three hard beats, a brief lull. Four beats and another
teasing pause. The shadows remain, circling like cautious invaders.
The wool blanket betrays its warmth, stinging her to

movement. Fresh from manoeuvres, he pins her with slumbering ease.
She stares down at his dark limb, so solid against her own skin.
The gap between them widens as she counts off each year in her mind.
He snorts, rolls onto his back. A streetlight eclipses his profile.
Free of his touch, she retreats to the hazy comfort of nicotine.
Deep breaths, measured and slow. She closes her
eyes to the shadows, finding a clearer form of darkness.

Time slips back by hours. Once more his fingers dance the
thin wires. His whisper coaxes beauty from a motorcycle ballad.
Tiny flickers fill the air, like shards of Cupid's updated arsenal.
The radiator beats a fresh refrain, startled fingers drop the
smouldering butt. Catch it up before the fire; hold the ember
until it fades. Paper and ash, afloat in last night's beer.
She steps tenderly through the glowing dark, back to the edge.
Rain so steady it coats the glass; soft light shears the veil.
The scent of him rises like spice. She leans close to taste his ear.
Reaction is instant—an aerial turn propelled by instinct. She feels
his wide, fearful stare but can't see past his upraised shaking fist.

Last Hunt Over Bras d'Or

From your perch on a dead spruce limb,
you watch the low sun cross the sky, slip
behind cold, burning hills and paint the lakes
as gold as their name. The dying season comes
late this year, held back by unseasonable warmth.
More prey for the watchful, like you and your
banded brethren. More time before wintering flocks
crowd the spruce and vie for carrion while the
freshest morsels hide beneath the whitened earth.

Elvis Clones

Somewhere, out there,
Elvis clones
Tag and bag
Bigfoot's babies
And the odd pile of ghost droppings.
Why else do you think
There are so many sightings?

Unless, by chance, he's
Tooling through time and space,
Riding shotgun for H.G.
Wells—or maybe they're
One and the same.
They've never been
Seen together.

What about Santa?
Can't beat a beard for disguise
And besides,
Check out that black belt,
Wider than the distance
Between the King and his next meal.
Vegas would be proud if it had a clue.

Stop the presses.
Sources close to Presley's pool boy
Strongly imply that maybe
The Donald™ bought the
Desiccated upper lip,
Permanently curled and mounted
On black velvet.

Thin Wires

You begin the romantic seduction,
Whispered amid starlight candle glows.
Strong, gentle fingers caress the neck and
Dance on thin wires, tempting the fall.

My heart beats to your shifting rhythm,
Teased into tune by an invisible hand.
Transient hazels meet summer-sky blues;
Thin wires bridge the distance we share.

A slight echoed sigh breaks the cadence,
As a new song is written and joined:
A duet of heartache and passion,
Held to the moment by thin wires.

Closer Now

Dawn
Echoes
Each
Thunder
clap and boom
under
grey
shadows;
the rumbles
feel closer now
than at dusk,
roll on
far
longer,
a buffer
against
heat
yet to
rise.

Baddeck

Anchored sailboats drift in slow
circles like shackled prisoners.
Parked sleeves bear names
instead of numbers. Moral Majority lies
just ahead of High Society. Very yar.
A yellow hull jumps out from the rest,
most of them white as the sun-kissed ripples.
Only one in ten even seems to move.
More feet pound docks than decks
in this saltwater haven, lakes
wrapped in a Highland embrace.
Masts come here to ease their burdens,
afloat on Bridget's tears. Inland, permanent
dwellers welcome visitors beneath
brightly lit exit signs. High-season
profits must last through the low.
I'm one of the passers-through,
staying longer than some but with
words of farewell just as firmly
lodged on the roof of my mouth.
One click of my tongue and they'll
drop, sliding like a dry-docked
boat to meet the tide.

Supplication

The furtive sun
sips from the shallow
well where once it
gulped, while shaded

clouds drag the winds
before them. Leaves
spread skyward in
wounded

supplication.
Scattered
droplets
fall like

unanswered
prayers on a
dwindling
congregation.

The Night She Left

She called me a beast
but she had the claws
Only used them on me
once, the night she left,
glaring behind her
oversized shades
and wrapped in

overreaction
Couldn't admit the truth
Not my fault
She found someone else
I know she did
But she'll be back
Look at all the stuff

she left behind
The sewing kit,
motherless
in a nest of torn blouses
Last night's dishes,
sunk like an oily wreck
The silks and furs I had to give,
hanging headless
like ghosts of past loves

Wisdom Flowers

In the age of gods
Quinquatria
Shadowed March's Ides
A day of peace

Offset by four of blood
Like scattered rubies
Minerva overcome by Mars

Yet even on a battlefield
Tiger lilies bloom
Lance-like leaves a testament
Heads bowed in remorse
Crimson tears a vow
Perennial wisdom

Dreamcatcher

fresh spun web
single strand
winds its way around the hoop,
crossing itself
over and over

diamonds cascade
between hoop and
jewelled heart, clustered
feathers form a draped triangle
meant for magic, ward against
darker dreams

leather, string, wood, plastic
maybe the feathers are real
leather smells of newness
speaks of something older
alarm, allure, flight, fight
snared nightmares
block the light

Window on a Taos Day

Past adobe roofs and struggling trees,
Higher than snow-topped Taos peak,
Fragments of sky dance and tease.
Past adobe roofs and struggling trees,
Clouds carry thoughts on the breeze
And invite words from my pen to seek
Past adobe walls and surrounding trees,
Higher than snow-topped Taos peak.

Mist

Fine mist drifts
on dawning air
like an astringent
wash, cleansing

past the surface.
Prismatic dancers
whisper kisses, luring you up
from the concrete.
Join in the swirl,
circle

and bow. Lift up
your face, eyes
closed and spirit
open. Here's beauty
no mirror can hold
for fear of skimming

so close but never
touching. Stirring,
you lick the dew
from your teeth.

The Last Time I Saw Lisa

The last time I saw Lisa, her hair flowed like
wheat in a tornado, obscuring her eyes, wiping
away tears faster than they could fall. Shallow
smiles grew to laughter, a sound so hard

I flinched. She lifted her hands as if to reach me,
spread her arms wide as if to forgive every
mistake made in the name of love, then

slipped into the clammy embrace of harbour
fog that swirled like faded dreams
beneath the over-bearing weight of
wrought iron and cement.

Evening Sounds

The early evening sun flickers
through one small window. Young
spring leaves on the nearest tree
glisten as the wind shifts them
in and out of the glow. Sunlight
dribbles diamonds and filigreed
leaves through lace. Unseen

evening sounds converge. Distant
vehicles rumble farther. Base-
board heaters crack and groan.
Dogs compete with the untried
musician next door, but his
piano always wins, if only on

beauty and purpose. The subtle
touch of cool air on my knees
as the wind parts the curtains
ever so slightly. We dance to virgin
refrains and listen for the coming
night. The wind whispers
phrases here and there,
if we stop to listen.

Knowledge and Memory

winged aspects of a one-eyed god
ravens cast over the earth
cast shadows black
as wing and head—
one for knowledge
one for memory—
together, etch their findings
across the minds of history
like quills fresh from deep black wells
across the barren page

Seaforth on the Atlantic

red-
orange sun
dips
into
horizon
yacht slips
off
trailing
persistent
hum in its wake
mingled with
wind-born
waves
breaking
foam nimble
fingers
play
over
stones

Scrape, Rattle, Bang

Monday night and the familiar
scrape rattle bang of pilfered
shopping carts beyond drawn
curtains. Again as the morning sun
cuts across rooftops, devouring
shadows and exposing residue.
Blue bags gutted and trampled,
left for the weekly truck that lumbers
along a grey street, gathering stripped
remains too lowly even for the night.

Grandfather Waltzes

Sweet-smelling pipe smoke drifting and
Dancing round your nimbus of hair,
Crooked fingers that beckon the mind
To the past, all soft as worn flannel, once
Green as young fir, a nesting place for
Wood shavings and dust, lost remnants of
Your craft, which claimed its ounce of flesh,
Devoured by the buzzing saw, no loss

Compared to her, your beloved Mary,
Survivor of twelve but too weak for
One more, the baby in the shoebox,
Tucked behind the stove for warmth,
Not enough, not mother's arms, Mary's
Arms, no more embrace near fifty years,

Until that final Valentine, your heart too
Strong to live without love, eyes blind to
All but her, you reached out for her waiting
Hands and danced her back to Heaven.

Fallen Seasons

Copper, ochre and mandarin
shades surround me in my sleep,
feeding dreams of fallen
seasons. Fetally recessed
in the warm hollow of mother's
quilt, I hide from September's chill,
hide from the grief
revived by his birthday
so soon after his death.
Big brother, gone
so long, now
forever.

Unfinished Portrait

Five years, to the day, since I
set aside my brush.
Shoved the half-finished canvas
in an unmarked
box. Three apartments
since then. One reason
or another. Moving
so the walls won't
crush me. Your face in my
memory, pressing out.
Every day, walls a little
closer, your face a little larger.

Today, I lean my two-legged
easel into the corner and
release the buried canvas.
Your image smiles,
features muted as if through a veil.
Chestnut curls brush
cheek and brow. Head
tilted as if awaiting
an answer, even now.
The eyes are wrong—set
too high, but more.
Pupils and irises still
a wash of burnt umber.
As flat as the last
look you gave me,
five years ago.

Magenta Skin

Magenta skin around
my eyes; something wicked
to remember him by. So many
secrets, no
release—emotion
wrapped inside
an ache—barren
landscape without
and within. No joy
cast on the unseen
path, no direction
left to follow.

Light Bright on High

Stars
swallow
night's
darkness
high above
back roads.
Bright
patterns
form on black
like a child's toy.
More timeless
than youth
and
sharper
than beauty.
The stars
count
on our
dreams.

White Feathers

Benign flyers on featherless wings
plunged without will into unsuspecting hearts;
stalwarts crumble to the ground, piece by
peace, like doves from a poisoned sky

Surfer Joe

Each day you roll
past on your spindly bike
weaving along the pebbled road,
your vision
straight as a spoke.

Where do your eyes lead? Away
from your smoke-grey shack and red-
blanket curtain over plastic
pane.

You first appeared
a twilight apparition
draped in rough crimson,
leaning on your sill
as I hid behind mine.

You still don't see me.

Your eyes must aim inward,
back to the beached '60's,
counting on waves for an afternoon
trip. Weed in the night
carried your dreams of water-
wheels rolling

until the air leaked out.
They couldn't hold the path like you
or swallow the salt-water
vow. Ten years
spent waiting then selling
what little you had
for a Florida reunion
of one.

Sold out, you crawled back
home. Abandoned
vans and soft-hearted neighbours
held you loosely.

Now you ride by like a desert surfer,
in and out on the hour.
If I follow you out, where
will I find you? Alone
on the dock, watching
your weed-greyed

reflection. A derelict
boat wallows in the shallows,
engine rusted and
bones slowly
crushed
in a negligent embrace.

Listening Post
A Tribute to the Cable Station at Hazel Hill, Nova Scotia

Stone-block monument in peeling yellow paint,
Valued only as a child's landmark—almost home.
The station remembers those who'll never be home,
Hears operators cursing God and praying to the saints.

The click of the wire still skitters through the walls.
Dot-dash strings made feeble lifelines, too weak
To keep the maiden from the salt-chill of the deep.
Her sunken corridors echo down the building's halls.

Newsreels made no mention (guess the writers never knew)
Of the Nova Scotia listening post touched before the rest.
Who ever heard of Hazel Hill? New York would have to do
As the helpless hero beating at his breast.
The yellow station went back to work again,
First link on the low end of the chain.

Restoration Piece

The dresser sits in the bedroom
corner, six months, like a cut
refusing to heal. Pitted
layers of varnish and paint

suppress the bare wood.
"Keep it. I don't want it."
He wasn't just talking
about the dresser. Her

only uncluttered space.
Relic and representation,
kept for sake of promises
made and dismissed

on a whim. Driving home,
she stops off for
scraper and solvent, brushes and paint
left for another

day. New knobs of brass,
goose-neck lamp, electric
screwdriver with instructions
on the back of the card.

Holiday weekend:
extra day's grace;
Extra-Strength Tylenol; two
more trips to Canadian Tire.

In less than a week
the goose sports a nylon
scarf and the brass gets buffed
by Hanes Her Way.

Monarch

monarch
vivid and true
in kaleidoscope robes
do you envy the hummingbird
his blur?

Born in Black

Born in black. From shirt and pants to
hair and eyes. You're even dark of skin, a tan
immune to the whims of Maritime sun. Not
from around here. (I slap at the buzzing
wasp in my head.) Nothing foreign but your
features. So much for my theory that swarthy
equals exotic and attractive. You look like
all the other guys, dragging back to work
empty handed, cigarettes hidden in the
black hole of your jeans.

Born in black. You'll die in black, swallowed
by the tar that chokes your lungs, another
black-death statistic. Who will you leave
behind? A pretty wife, plump with child?
Wed in haste, you took the first job offered—
call centre cog in a cold stone tower. Half a B.A.
prepared you for this, or the midnight shift at a
corner Green Gables. They robbed it last night.
Men in black, pockets full of cash and arms
filled with cartons of filtered tobacco.

For the Lost

The wind howls outside
my pane, sadness
in each gust for the lost,
the forgotten, whose names
fade on weathered stones,
beaten smooth by the wind
outside my pane.

No Sparks

We buy a house on a quiet
street where neighbours orbit
our lives like elliptic comets

A high stone fence all around
in case one of them crashes

A chesterfield in forest green,
matching chairs beside;
no loveseat but marble hugs
the fireplace—caged heat

No sparks fly

Hot air spews from the dryer vent
while I hug the vibrating washer,
envy its simple dance and long
to follow the rushing air

You hide in your makeshift bodega,
caress each bottle as you once did me
when my figure whetted your taste

No dust settles on your little loves

Clinging vines creep
over whitewash trellis,
pernicious as gossip,
emanate along cedar shingles and
shakes

Annie Laurie's Parting Gift

Name barely remembered
Face long forgotten
Removed by years and
Miles, crisscrossing the country
From job to job,

One tentative life to the next
Running from her youth
The family left behind
Distance and silence
Broken

At last by death
Bringing strangered kin
Together to divide
Her life's shattered,
Scattered worth

Fishing!

Wading wet and wobbly along the winding
River, reaching past restrictions and railing
Against the atrocities of angling in April.
How did I happen upon such a hobby? I hate
Fishing! Fetching water and wood, swatting flies,
Squatting in shrubs and spraying my shoes,
Cursing the conceit that caused me to come
On this overnight odyssey. It can't be over
Quick enough. Qualms and questions all quelled.
Men—no matter how handsome—don't merit misery.

William Shakespeare, Astronaut

For all the magic grace of words
Strung end to end in flawless line
I would not trade the endless night
For any straight or slanted rhyme

Whether thought be swift and fluid
Soaring like nature's free-winged fowl
Or stiff as manmade metal flyers
Matters not to one above them all

The clouds part as velvet curtains
As stars shine down, pin point on cue
One for each fretting face below
Turned upward in ignorant awe

As I walk upon breathless night
Strutting player bereft of sound
For all the world, an audience
To this, my hour upon the stage

At the Outset

ouroboros dreams the night
illuminated
aurora borealis slithers
freer
teasing Gaia's senses
one bite
inflicting conceptual fantasy
laboured
afterbirth rains down like
ripe apples

www.ingramcontent.com/pod-product-compliance
Lightning Source LLC
Chambersburg PA
CBHW061258040426
42444CB00010B/2411